Desert Animals

Siân Smith

Raintree is an imprint of Capstone Global Library Limited, a company incorporated in England and Wales having its registered office at 7 Pilgrim Street, London, EC4V 6LB – Registered company number: 6695582

www.raintreepublishers.co.uk
myorders@raintreepublishers.co.uk

Edited by Sian Smith and Diyan Leake
Designed by Marcus Bell
Picture research by Tracy Cummins
Production by Helen McCreath
Originated by Capstone Global Library Ltd
Printed and bound in China

ISBN 978 1 406 28067 8
18 17 16 15 14
10 9 8 7 6 5 4 3 2 1

British Library Cataloguing in Publication Data
Smith, Sian.
Desert animals. -- (Animal in their habitats)
A full catalogue record for this book is available from the British Library.

Acknowledgements
We would like to thank the following people for permission to reproduce photographs: Alamy p. 5 (© Rick & Nora Bowers); Getty Images p. 15 (Tier Und Naturfotografie J und C Sohns); istockphoto pp. 8 (© Vrouwenhof21nl), 14, 22b (© ElementalImaging); Science Source pp. 11 (Suzanne L. Collins), 18 (Dan Suzio), 19 (James Steinberg), 22a (Dan Suzio); Shutterstock pp. 6 (EcoPrint), 7 (efendy), 9 (gracious_tiger), 10 (visuelldesign), 12 (nattanan726), 13 (raulbaenacasado), 16 (Stacey Ann Alberts), 20a (Lukasz Janyst), 20b (szefei), 20c (Galyna Andrushko), 20d (2009fotofriends); Superstock pp. 4 (imagebroker.net), 17 (NHPA), 21 (Animals Animals).

Cover photograph of meerkat babies in the Kalahari Desert, South Africa, reproduced with permission of Shutterstock (Ecoprint).

Back cover photograph reproduced with permission of Shutterstock (gracious_tiger).

We would like to thank Michael Bright for his invaluable help in the preparation of this book.

Every effort has been made to contact copyright holders of material reproduced in this book. Any omissions will be rectified in subsequent printings if notice is given to the publisher.

Contents

Animals in the desert

A kangaroo lives here.

A kangaroo rat lives here.

A meerkat lives here.

A scorpion lives here.

A camel lives here.

A lizard lives here.

A rattlesnake lives here.

A kingsnake lives here.

A fox lives here.

A vulture lives here.

A roadrunner lives here.

A coyote lives here.

A dung beetle lives here.

A sand cat lives here.

A goanna lives here.

A dingo lives here.

All about deserts

Deserts are very dry places. Many deserts are hot in the day and cold at night.

Can you spot the desert?

Answer: a

What am I?

I have two big feet to jump with.

I have a long tail.

I can keep food in my cheeks.

I am smaller than a meerkat.

Picture glossary

 goanna

 roadrunner

Index

22

Notes for teachers and parents

Before reading

Tuning in: Talk about what it must be like to live in a desert. What sort of animals might live in a hot, dry desert?

After reading

Recall and reflection: How do desert animals keep cool? (Many hide underground in the heat of the day and come out at night when it is cooler.)

Sentence knowledge: Help the child to count the number of words in each sentence.

Word knowledge (phonics): Challenge the child to find an animal beginning with *k* on p. 4 and an animal beginning with *m* on p. 6.

Word recognition: Challenge the child to race you to point at the word *here* on any page.

Rounding off

Say the following rhyme together:

Three friendly meerkats wondering what to do.
One hid underground and then there were two.
Two friendly meerkats sitting in the sun.
One hid underground and then there was one.
One lonely meerkat sitting in the sun.
He hid underground and then there were none.

Word coverage

Topic words
camel
coyote
desert
dingo
dung beetle
fox
iguana
kangaroo
kingsnake
lizard
meerkat
rattlesnake
roadrunner
sand cat
scorpion
vulture

High-frequency words
a
all
here
in
the

Sentence stem
A _____ lives here.

Ask children to read these words:
kangaroo   p. 4
rat   p. 5
meerkat   p. 6
sand cat   p. 17